Brilliant Support Activities

# Word Level Work – Vocabulary

Irene Yates

**Brilliant**
PUBLICATIONS

We hope you and your class enjoy using this book. Other books in the Brilliant Support Activities series include:

**Language titles**

| | |
|---|---|
| Word Level Work – Phonics | 978 1 897675 32 8 |
| Sentence Level Work | 978 1 897675 33 5 |
| Text Level Work | 978 1 903853 00 9 |

**Science titles**

| | |
|---|---|
| Understanding Living Things | 978 1 897675 59 5 |
| Understanding Materials | 978 1 897675 60 1 |
| Understanding Physical Processes | 978 1 897675 61 8 |

Published by Brilliant Publications
Unit 10, Sparrow Hall Farm, Edlesborough, Dunstable LU6 2ES, UK
Tel:      01525 222292
Fax:      01525 222720
email:    info@brilliantpublications.co.uk
website:  www.brilliantpublications.co.uk

The name Brilliant Publications and the logo are registered trademarks.

Written by Irene Yates
Cover designed by Small World Design
Illustrated by Lynda Murray

Printed in the UK.

# Contents

# Introduction to the series

The Brilliant Support Activities series contains four language titles designed to give reinforcement to pupils who are finding it difficult to keep up with the skills and concepts in the National Literacy Strategy. The four books are closely linked:

- Word Level Work – Vocabulary
- Word Level Work – Phonics
- Sentence Level Work
- Text Level Work

Each book contains 42 photocopiable ideas for use with Key Stage 2 pupils who are working at levels consistent with the first four years of the National Literacy Strategy document. The activities are presented in an age-appropriate manner and provide a flexible, but structured, resource for teaching pupils to understand all the concepts that are introduced in the Literacy Hour during reception, Y1, Y2 and Y3.

The tasks in the books are kept short and snappy, to facilitate concentration. The vocabulary used is especially focused on the lists of high frequency and medium frequency words that the children are to be taught as sight recognition words during the National Literacy Strategy. The pages have a clear layout and the text has been kept to a minimum so that struggling readers can cope. To ensure that the instructions are easy to follow, the following logos have been used to indicate different types of activity:

 What to do

 Think and do

 Read

 Help

Many pupils begin to feel disaffected when they find abstract language concepts hard to grasp. The activities in this series are designed, with information and questioning, to foster understanding and to help those pupils to experience success and achievement. The expectation that the pupil will achieve will help to build confidence, competence and self-esteem which, in turn, will foster learning.

# Introduction to the book

The activity pages are designed to support and consolidate the work you do during the Literacy Hour. They are intended to add to your pupils' knowledge and understanding of how the English language works.

The book contains activities that work on concepts of syntax, punctuation and vocabulary that are introduced during the first four years of the National Literacy Strategy. Many of these concepts are quite abstract and require lots of reinforcement before they are understood. Some pupils, who find the rules of English difficult to understand, actually have greater success with deconstructing and fragmenting the language and learning how it works in an analytical way, with constant reinforcements, than by using it in a functional mode, through talking and writing. Learning about vocabulary and grammar in this way gives the pupils the tools to be able to talk about and understand language development.

The sheets can be used with individual children, pairs or very small groups, as the need arises. The text on the pages has been kept as short as possible, so that reluctant or poorer readers will not feel swamped by 'words on the page'. For the same reason we have used white space, boxes and logos, to help the pupils to understand the sheets easily, and to give them a measure of independence in working through them.

It is not the author's intention that a teacher should expect all the children to complete all the sheets. Rather that the sheets be used with a flexible approach, so that the book will provide a bank of resources that will meet needs as they arise. Many of the sheets can be modified and extended in very simple ways.

# Think about the alphabet

## Read

This is the alphabet in capital letters:

A B C D E F G H I J K L M N O P Q R S T U V W X Y Z

## What to do

Say the alphabet aloud.

Continue these rows as far as you can.

Q  R  S  T  U

D  E  F  G  H

J  K  L  M

M  N  O  P

H  I  J  K

## Think and do

Write in capitals.

Which letter comes before I?

Which letter comes before P?

Which letter comes after S?

Which letter comes after G?

Which letter comes between I and K?

Which letter comes between N and P?

Which letters come between Q and T?

Which letters come between J and M?

# Letters, letters, letters

## Read
This is the alphabet in lower case letters:

**a b c d e f g h i j k l m n o p q r s t u v w x y z**

## What to do
Say their sounds, then say the alphabet aloud.

Continue these rows as far as you can.

d   e   f   g   h

l   m   n   o   p

o   p   q   r   s

q   r   s   t   u

g   h   i   j   k

## Think and do
Write in lower case letters.

Which letter comes before b?

Which letter comes before k?

Which letter comes after g?

Which letter comes after w?

Which letter comes between m and o?

Which letter comes between r and t?

Which letters come between w and z?

Which letters come between e and j?

# Make them BIG

## What to do
Write these words in **CAPITAL** letters.

ant     ANT            net

bag                      odd

cat                      pet

dear                   queen

end                      ran

fat                      sad

girl                     tea

her                      us

if                       vest

jam                     went

key                     X-mas

lip                      yellow

mud                    zip

## What to do
Write these words in **small** letters.

| | | | |
|---|---|---|---|
| APE | ape | NUT | |
| BIG | | OLD | |
| CAR | | PEN | |
| DOG | | QUACK | |
| EGG | | RED | |
| FIT | | SIT | |
| GOT | | TOP | |
| HAT | | UP | |
| ICE | | VAN | |
| JIG | | WAS | |
| KICK | | X-RAY | |
| LID | | YOU | |
| MAN | | ZERO | |

## Read
The first letter of a word is called the 'initial' letter.

## What to do
Finish the sentences.
Use the words in the box.

A is for a

B is for b

C is for c

D is for d

E is for e

F is for f

G is for g

H is for h

I is for i

**Choose from these words. Look for the initial letter.**

| hill | and | do |
|------|-----|-----|
| far  | big | go  |
| cap  | ear | it  |

## Read

The first letter of a word is called the 'initial' letter.

## What to do

Finish the sentences.
Use the words in the box.

J is for j

K is for k

L is for l

M is for m

N is for n

O is for o

P is for p

Q is for q

R is for r

---

**Choose from these words. Look for the initial letter.**

| like | jam | mum |
|------|-----|-----|
| kiss | on | ran |
| no | queen | play |

---

## Read

The first letter of a word is called the 'initial' letter.

## What to do

Finish the sentences.
Use the words in the box.

S is for s

T is for t

U is for u

V is for v

W is for w

X is for x

Y is for y

Z is for z

---

**Choose from these words. Look for the initial letter.**

| yes | we | zero |
|-----|------|------|
| to  | said | us   |
| very | x-ray | |

---

# Initial sounds

## Read
Instead of looking for the initial letter, this time we are looking at the initial *sound*. In these words, two letters make *one* sound.

## What to do
Finish the sentences.
Use the words in the box.

Ch is for ch

Ch is for ch

Ch is for ch

Sh is for sh

Sh is for sh

Sh is for sh

Th is for th

Th is for th

Th is for th

| Choose from these words. Look for the initial sound. | | |
| --- | --- | --- |
| she | the | chip |
| this | chin | they |
| shape | show | chick |

## Read

These *animal* words are in alphabetical order.

ant
bear
cow
deer
elephant
fox

## What to do

These animal words are not in alphabetical order.
Make a new list, putting all the words into alphabetical order.

kangaroo          parrot
rat               zebra
insect            jackal
~~ape~~           owl
unicorn           ~~bird~~
tiger             sheep
dog               hyena
mouse             worm
emu               quail
vulture           natterjack
lion              fox
yak               gnu
~~cat~~

ape
bird
cat

## Think and do

One letter of the alphabet is missing. Which letter is it? _____
Why do you think it is missing?

**A B C D E F G H I J K L M N O P Q R S T U V W X Y Z**

## What to do

Put these words into alphabetical order:

| dog | girl |
|-----|------|
| ant | zebra |
| football | horse |

## Read

It is easy if none of the words begin with the same letter.

This is what you do if some words begin with the same letter, like **dog** and **dish**. They both begin with 'd'. Cover the 'd' and look at the next letter:

d̸og          d̸ish

**I** comes before **O** in the alphabet, so 'di' comes before 'do'.

What about **hand** and **horse**? Cover the 'h' and you have:

h̸and          h̸orse

**A** comes before **O**, so 'ha' comes before 'ho'.

## What to do

Put these words into alphabetical order:

| bed | | much | | seen | |
|-----|--|------|--|------|--|
| back | | made | | saw | |
| but | | more | | slip | |

| her | | time | |
|-----|--|------|--|
| had | | three | |
| how | | take | |

# Numbers

## Read

| | | | |
|---|---|---|---|
| 1 | one | first | 1st |
| 2 | two | second | 2nd |
| 3 | three | third | 3rd |
| 4 | four | fourth | 4th |
| 5 | five | fifth | 5th |
| 6 | six | sixth | 6th |
| 7 | seven | seventh | 7th |
| 8 | eight | eighth | 8th |
| 9 | nine | ninth | 9th |
| 10 | ten | tenth | 10th |
| 11 | eleven | eleventh | 11th |
| 12 | twelve | twelfth | 12th |
| 13 | thirteen | thirteenth | 13th |
| 14 | fourteen | fourteenth | 14th |
| 15 | fifteen | fifteenth | 15th |

## What to do

Fill in this table:

| 1 | one | first | 1st |
|---|---|---|---|
| | | | |
| | three | | |
| | | | |
| 5 | | | |
| | | | |
| | | | |
| | | | |
| | | | |
| | | | |
| | | | 10th |
| | | | |
| | | twelfth | |

www.brilliantpublications.co.u

# Which month?

## Read

| | |
|---|---|
| 1st | January |
| 2nd | February |
| 3rd | March |
| 4th | April |
| 5th | May |
| 6th | June |
| 7th | July |
| 8th | August |
| 9th | September |
| 10th | October |
| 11th | November |
| 12th | December |

**Useful phrases**
last month
this month
next month

## What to do
Finish these sentences:

This month is _____ .

Last month was _____ .

Next month will be _____ .


The fourth month is _____ .

The eighth month is _____ .

The month before October is _____ .

The month after June is _____ .

If it is September now, last month was _____ .

If it was May last month, this month is _____ .

The month after the 9th month is _____ .

The last month of the year is _____ .

# Months of the year

## Read

There are 12 months in a year:

| first | 1st | January |
|-------|-----|---------|
| second | 2nd | February |
| third | 3rd | March |
| fourth | 4th | April |
| fifth | 5th | May |
| sixth | 6th | June |
| seventh | 7th | July |
| eighth | 8th | August |
| ninth | 9th | September |
| tenth | 10th | October |
| eleventh | 11th | November |
| twelfth | 12th | December |

## What to do

Fill in the columns:

| January | first | 1st |
|---------|-------|-----|
|  |  | 2nd |
|  |  |  |
| April |  |  |
|  |  |  |
|  | sixth |  |
|  |  |  |
|  |  |  |
|  |  |  |
|  |  |  |
|  |  |  |
|  |  |  |

# Which day?

## Read

| | |
|---|---|
| 1st | Sunday |
| 2nd | Monday |
| 3rd | Tuesday |
| 4th | Wednesday |
| 5th | Thursday |
| 6th | Friday |
| 7th | Saturday |

**Useful phrases**
last week
this week
next week

## What to do
Finish these sentences:

Today is ———————————— .

Yesterday was ———————————— .

Tomorrow will be ———————————— .

The third day of the week is ———————————— .

The sixth day of the week is ———————————— .

The day before the 2nd day is ———————————— .

The last day of the week is ———————————— .

If it is Monday today, tomorrow will be ———————————— .

If it was Thursday yesterday, tomorrow will be ———————————— .

# Word lists

## Read

Here are some words for you to read:

| | | | |
|---|---|---|---|
| and | you | them | she |
| for | many | cat | see |
| once | this | pull | time |
| will | are | big | that |

## What to do

Put all the three-letter words in one list.

What will be the heading for the other list?

| Three-letter words | |
|---|---|
| | |

## Think and do

Score 2 points for every word you can read and write.

Have you scored 32? If not, try again!

## Read

Here are some words for you to read:

| | | | |
|---|---|---|---|
| jump | there | love | night |
| house | took | water | last |
| would | came | when | your |
| name | were | three | about |

## What to do

Put all the four-letter words in one list.

What will be the heading for the other list?

| Four-letter words | |
|---|---|
| | |

## Think and do

Score 2 points for every word you can read and write.

Have you scored 32? If not, try again!

## What to do

Do this puzzle. Look at the words in the box and read the clues.

Rhymes with:

Jack

boy

mother

said

day

pair

tool

mouse

wood

right

be

blister

hat

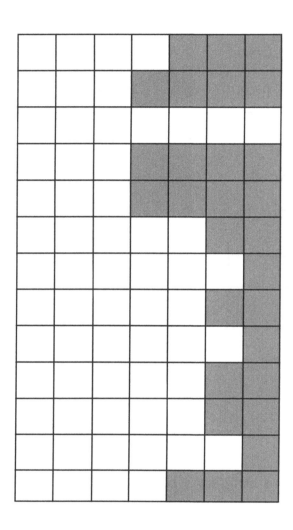

| brother | way | where | sister | should |
|---------|-----|-------|--------|--------|
| back | toy | house | that | |
| school | night | three | bed | |

This sheet may be photocopied for use by the purchasing institution only.

www.brilliantpublications.co.uk

## What to do
Find the word in the sentence.
Draw a line under it.

| | |
|---|---|
| I | <u>I</u> like to play. |
| up | I am going up the stairs. |
| look | We look for my dad. |
| we | Will we see my dad? |
| like | I like the dog. |
| on | One day we went on a bus. |
| at | We got off at my nan's. |
| for | We went for tea. |

## Think and do
Write the words here:

## Help
Say the words to yourself as you write.

© Irene Yates
Word Level Work – Vocabulary

## What to do

Find the word in the sentence.
Draw a line under it.

| | |
|---|---|
| and | The dog and I play. |
| up | We go up the stairs. |
| look | We look for my dad. |
| we | Will we see him? |
| like | I like my dad. |
| on | We sit on the stairs and wait. |
| at | Here is my dad, at last. |
| for | He says, "Are you waiting for me?" |

## Think and do

Write the words here:

## Help

Say the words to yourself as you write.

## What to do
Find the word in the sentence.
Draw a line under it.

| | |
|---|---|
| is | Here <u>is</u> my dad. |
| he | He said we can go out. |
| go | Maybe we can go to the park. |
| you | "I would like to go to the park with you," |
| | said Dad. |
| this | I'm glad we are going this morning. |
| going | After the park, we're going to my cousins' house for tea. |
| they | They will be pleased to see us. |

## Think and do
Write the words here:

## Help
Say the words to yourself as you write.

# Vowels and consonants

## Read

There are 26 letters in the alphabet. Only five of them are vowels:

All the other letters are consonants. Every word in English, except for 'hymn' and 'rhythm', has at least one vowel in it.

## What to do

How many vowels are in 'fight'?_____     Write the vowels here: _____

How many vowels are in 'choose'?_____     Write the vowels here: _____

Are there three vowels in 'horrible'?_____

How many letters are in 'early'?_____     Write the vowels here: _____

How many letters are in 'needle'? _____     Write the vowels here: _____

Are there four vowels in 'skateboard'? _____

Which vowels are in 'bicycle'?  _____

## Think and do

Write the five vowels here:

Write the 21 consonants here:

# Hidden words

## Read

Some words have other words hidden inside them.
Can you spot the small words in these words?
Draw a ring round the small words.

p(on)d      soft      lift      match

sand      wink      fish      last

| **Small words** | | |
|---|---|---|
| an | if | at |
| of | in | is |
| as | on | |

## What to do

A three-letter word is hidden in each of these words.

s(oak)      grate      steal      beggar      clipper

scarf      plant      champion      shears      scowl

Find the words and write them in the boxes. The clues will help.

a tree = **oak**

an insect =

kind of transport =

what a hen lays =

a rodent =

part of your mouth =

meat =

a bird =

something to drink =

what you hear with =

## Read

Some words are made by joining two together.
For example:

|       |   |       |   |          |
|-------|---|-------|---|----------|
| arm   | + | chair | = | armchair |
| air   | + | port  | = | airport  |

## What to do

Read these words:

| | | | |
|---|---|---|---|
| bed   | bin  | bag  | light |
| foot  | man  | ~~mill~~ | dust  |
| house | hand | bell | snow  |
| door  | room | ball | ~~wind~~ |

Make some new words:

| wind | + | mill | = | windmill |
|------|---|------|---|----------|
|      | + |      | = |          |
|      | + |      | = |          |
|      | + |      | = |          |
|      | + |      | = |          |
|      | + |      | = |          |
|      | + |      | = |          |
|      | + |      | = |          |
|      | + |      | = |          |

## Help

We call the new words 'compound' words.

# Similar words

## Read
Some words mean almost the same as other words.
For example:

    a **big** dog   a **large** dog

The words **big** and **large** mean nearly the same.

## What to do
Read each word and write another that is similar in meaning.

small

talk

begin

tug

crawl

gift

end

look

## Help
Choose from these words:

    start      speak      present      pull

    creep      finish      watch      little

Word Level Work – Vocabulary

# 'Not' words – contractions

## Read

Sometimes we join the word 'not' on to another word.
We leave out the 'o' and put an apostrophe (') in its place.

For example:     do not  ⟶  don't

## What to do

Follow the rule to join these words together:

does not  ⟶

was not  ⟶

are not  ⟶

has not  ⟶

have not  ⟶

is not  ⟶

were not  ⟶

would not  ⟶

could not  ⟶

might not  ⟶

cannot  ⟶                    (Hint: this one is a bit different!)

## Think and do

Write what you think happens to these words:

am not [ ]     shall not [ ]     will not [ ]

(Clue: the words change.)

## Help

These words are called 'contractions'.

## Read

Some words have an initial letter that you don't hear when you say the word.
The silent letters are usually:

| For example: | gnat | ⟶ | we say | *nat* |
| | knew | ⟶ | we say | *new* |
| | psalm | ⟶ | we say | *salm* |
| | wrap | ⟶ | we say | *rap* |

## What to do

Put the silent letters in front of these words to make them complete.

| **We say:** | **The word is:** |
| --- | --- |
| *nife* | |
| *rist* | |
| *terodactyl* | |
| *nome* | |
| *rite* | |
| *nash* | |
| *nee* | |
| *nock* | |
| *narl* | |
| *reck* | |

## Help

There are    3 'silent g' words
            3 'silent k' words
            1 'silent p' word
            3 'silent w' words

Irene Yates
Word Level Work – Vocabulary

## Read

Adjectives come in three ways:

| | | |
|---|---|---|
| Normative | – | tall |
| Comparative | – | taller |
| Superlative | – | tallest |

## What to do

Fill in the spaces.

| Normative | Comparative | Superlative |
|---|---|---|
| | | highest |
| | shorter | |
| old | | |
| wide | | |
| | | finest |
| ripe | | |
| | wiser | |
| | | tamest |
| pale | | |
| | sharper | |

Word Level Work – Vocabulary

www.brilliantpublications.co.uk

# Adding 'er' and 'est'

## Read

When we add 'er' and 'est' to some adjectives, we have to double the last letter. These are always words that end with a consonant coming after a vowel.

For example:

hot
(normative)

hotter
(comparative)

hottest
(superlative)

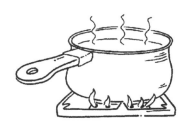

## What to do

Fill in the spaces, remembering the rule.

| Normative | Comparative | Superlative |
|-----------|-------------|-------------|
| hot | hotter | hottest |
|  | flatter |  |
|  |  | wettest |
| thin |  |  |
| sad |  |  |
|  | bigger |  |
|  | fitter |  |
|  |  | reddest |
| fat |  |  |

# Antonyms

## Read

These words are *opposite* in meanings:

| | | | | | |
|---|---|---|---|---|---|
| good | ⟷ | bad | open | ⟷ | shut |
| big | ⟷ | small | hard | ⟷ | soft |
| in | ⟷ | out | new | ⟷ | old |
| empty | ⟷ | full | strong | ⟷ | weak |

## What to do

Words that are opposites are called *antonyms*.
Write an antonym for each of these words:

early    late          pretty

tall                   dry

cold                   thin

tame                   give

bottom                 over

high                   start

## Read

To make a verb show the *past tense*, we add the 'ed' sound.
If the word ends with 'e', we only add 'd'.

For example:

Today I play *(now).* ——→ Yesterday I play**ed** *(past tense).*

Today I race *(now).* ——→ Yesterday I race**d** *(past tense).*

## What to do

Make each of these verbs show the past tense by adding 'd' or 'ed'.

| | | |
|---|---|---|
| move | add | bake |
| paint | work | tie |
| wipe | wave | rest |
| save | miss | sail |
| use | mix | tie |

## Help

A verb is a 'doing word'.

## Read

When we add 'ed' to some verbs, we have to double the last letter.

For example:

Today I hug my mum *(now)*.

Yesterday I hu**gg**ed my mum *(past tense)*.

Today I tap my pencil *(now)*.

Yesterday I ta**pp**ed my pencil *(past tense)*.

## What to do

Make each of these verbs show the past tense by doubling the last letter and adding 'ed'.

| hug | | tap | | plot | |
|-----|---|-----|---|------|---|

| clap | | wag | | nag | |
|------|---|-----|---|-----|---|

| stop | | chop | | jig | |
|------|---|------|---|-----|---|

| beg | | tip | | flap | |
|-----|---|-----|---|------|---|

| dip | | plan | | plug | |
|-----|---|------|---|------|---|

# The prefix 'un'

## Read

You can sometimes make the opposite of a word (its *antonym*)
by adding the prefix 'un'.

For example:     tidy ⟶ untidy

## What to do

Turn these words into words meaning their opposite, by adding the prefix 'un'.

happy

pack

load

wrap

do

kind

lock

tie

able

known

well

paid

## Help

A **prefix** is a group of letters that can be added at the *beginning*
of a root word to change it.

# The prefix 'dis'

## Read

You can sometimes make the opposite of a word (its *antonym*)
by adding the prefix 'dis'.

For example:      trust      ⟶      distrust

## What to do

Turn these words into words meaning their opposite, by adding the prefix 'dis'.

agree

appear

like

approve

honest

comfort

connect

order

able

obey

## Help

A **prefix** is a group of letters that can be added at the *beginning*
of a root word to change it.

# The prefix 're'

## Read

You can sometimes add the prefix 're' to a word to mean 'happening again'.

For example:     order  ⟶  reorder

## What to do

Change these words by adding the prefix 're'.

create

arrange

build

run

place

count

direct

address

call

set

join

open

## Help

A **prefix** is a group of letters that can be added at the *beginning* of a root word to change it.

This sheet may be photocopied for use by the purchasing institution only.
www.brilliantpublications.co.uk

# The suffix '-ful'

## Read

A **suffix** is a group of letters that can be added to the *end* of a word to change it. The suffix can change a noun into an adjective.

For example:     help *(noun)* ———➤ helpful *(adjective)*

care *(noun)* ———➤ careful *(adjective)*

## What to do

Change these nouns into adjectives by adding 'ful'.

grace

use

truth

spite

fright

colour

wonder

hope

joy

doubt

hurt

waste

## Help

A **suffix** comes at the *end* of a root word.

# The suffix '-ly'

## Read

A **suffix** is a group of letters that can be added to the end of a word to change it. The suffix 'ly' can change an adjective into an adverb.

For example:     quick *(adjective)* ⟶ quickly *(adverb)*

bright *(adjective)* ⟶ brightly *(adverb)*

## What to do

Change these adjectives into adverbs by adding 'ly'.

clear

quiet

slow

safe

proper

strong

soft

sudden

painful

perfect

strict

rare

## Help

A **suffix** comes at the *end* of a root word.

# The suffix '-less'

## Read

A **suffix** is a group of letters that can be added to the *end* of a word to change it. The suffix 'less' can change a noun into an adjective.

For example:  help *(noun)* ⟶ helpless *(adjective)*

care *(noun)* ⟶ careless *(adjective)*

## What to do

Change these nouns into adjectives by adding 'less'.

taste | use

joy | price

time | name

speech | sleep

thought | love

home | hope

## Help

A **suffix** comes at the *end* of a root word.

# Root words

## Read

Root words are the words we can add prefixes and suffixes to, when we want to make new words.

For example:    help *(root word)*    ⟶    *prefix*    *suffix*
un)help(ful

use *(root word)*    ⟶    use(less)    *suffix*

## What to do

Read these words carefully. Put their sections into the correct columns.

| kindness | unkindly | inside | outside |
| homeless | homework | disappear | appearance |
| comfortable | uncomfortable | dislike | likeable |

| Word | Root word | Prefix | Suffix |
|---|---|---|---|
| kindness | kind | | ness |
| | | | |
| | | | |
| | | | |
| | | | |
| | | | |
| | | | |

## Help

A **prefix** comes *before* the root word.
A **suffix** comes *after* the root word.

# Roots – making new words

## What to do

Read all the words below. Read all the prefixes and suffixes in the boxes. How many new words can you make? (You can make more than one word for most of the root words. Use a dictionary to help you.)

| | | | |
|---|---|---|---|
| kind | care | hope | truth |
| happy | mind | sense | direct |
| use | trust | count | agree |

**Prefixes**
un
dis
mis
non

**Suffixes**
ful
fully
ly
less
ment

## Help

You can add more prefixes and suffixes that you know to the lists.

## Read

If a noun is *singular*, it means there's only one.

If a noun is *plural*, it means there's more than one.

## What to do

Put these words into the correct group.

| | | | | |
|---|---|---|---|---|
| walks | baby | balloons | mothers | father |
| ladies | stories | morning | fights | places |
| bear | shoe | boots | brushes | home |
| porch | lunches | cross | harness | class |

| Singular | Plural |
|---|---|
|  |  |

# Plurals – adding 's'

## Read

We add 's' to some nouns to make them mean more than one.
Most of the nouns that end with 'e' just add an 's' to make them plural.

For example:     chocolate  ⟶  chocolates
                      shoe  ⟶  shoes

Many other nouns just add an 's', too.

For example:     girl  ⟶  girls
                      boy  ⟶  boys

## What to do

Add 's' to these nouns to make them plural:

dog         [        ]         bed       [        ]

leg         [        ]         door     [        ]

day         [        ]         house   [        ]

week      [        ]         night    [        ]

month    [        ]         school  [        ]

book      [        ]         sister   [        ]

ball       [        ]         tree    [        ]

name     [        ]         brother  [        ]

# Plurals – adding 'es'

## Read

Some nouns need 'es' instead of 's' to make them mean more than one.
These are mostly words that end with **ch**, **tch**, **s**, **sh**, **x** or **z**.

For example:

| | | |
|---|---|---|
| bench | ⟶ | benches |
| match | ⟶ | matches |
| bus | ⟶ | buses |
| brush | ⟶ | brushes |
| dress | ⟶ | dresses |
| fox | ⟶ | foxes |
| waltz | ⟶ | waltzes |

## What to do

Add 'es' to these nouns to make them plural:

coach    [ ]      box    [ ]

peach    [ ]      torch    [ ]

church    [ ]      pass    [ ]

crutch    [ ]      bench    [ ]

crash    [ ]      hutch    [ ]

bush    [ ]      pitch    [ ]

dish    [ ]      glass    [ ]

class    [ ]      guess    [ ]

## Read

There are two ways to make plurals out of nouns ending with 'y':
If there is a vowel before the 'y', just add 's'.

For example:     monk**e**y  *vowel*  ⟶     monkeys

If there is a consonant before the 'y', change the 'y' to 'i' and add 'es'.

For example:     ba**b**y  ⟶     babies
*consonant*

## What to do

Write the plurals of these words. Remember the rule and make it work.

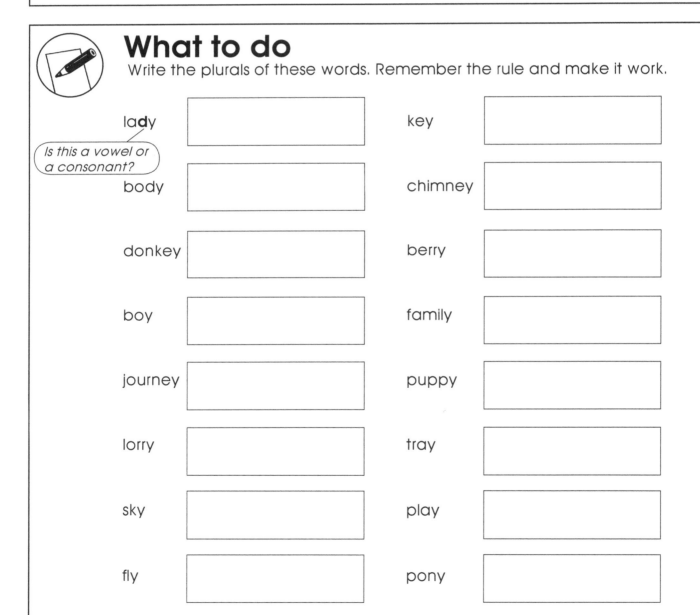

lady

*Is this a vowel or a consonant?*

body

donkey

boy

journey

lorry

sky

fly

key

chimney

berry

family

puppy

tray

play

pony

Lightning Source UK Ltd.
Milton Keynes UK
UKOW07f1807120616

276085UK00003B/77/P